"Finally, a prov

each of us as we navigate this journey called life. *You–An Ideal Woman* is an extraordinary book, a practical plan on how to 'choose life' so that you and your descendants might live. Written with grace and reverence, it is a book of empowerment through a delightful journey of discovery about ourselves as women and what we are called to be. *You–An Ideal Woman* is definitely a book that you will read again and again."

Robin La Moria, M.A.A.C.C.D
Family Minister, St. Vincent de Paul Parish,
Federal Way, Washington

"Practical! A model that will change you forever. *You– An Ideal Woman* is insightful—a learning for all women, married or unmarried. It will challenge your intellect and in every way. A stimulation of your inspirations, it is your manual for everyday life."

Ngozi T. Udoye, Ph.D.
Missionary and Researcher
Loyola University, Chicago

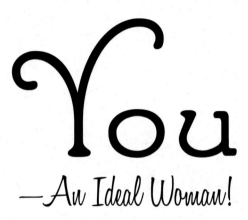

You

—An Ideal Woman!

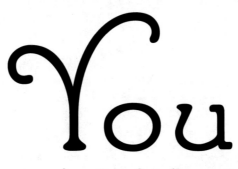

You
—An Ideal Woman!

by
Stella Ihuoma Nnanabu

BECOMING THE PROVERBS 31
WIFE AND MOTHER

TATE PUBLISHING & Enterprises

Published by Tate Publishing & Enterprises, LLC
127 E. Trade Center Terrace | Mustang, Oklahoma 73064 USA
1.888.361.9473 | www.tatepublishing.com

Tate Publishing is committed to excellence in the publishing industry. The company reflects the philosophy established by the founders, based on Psalm 68:11,
"The Lord gave the word and great was the company of those who published it."

Book design copyright © 2008 by Tate Publishing, LLC. All rights reserved.
Cover design by Kellie Southerland
Interior design by Kandi Evans

Published in the United States of America

ISBN: 978-1-60604-145-1
1. Christian Living: Practical Life: Women
2. Inspiration: Motivational: General Religious Inspiration
08.05.30

TABLE OF CONTENTS

DEDICATION

This book is prayerfully dedicated to the three most important women in my life, whom I admire affectionately and thank for their influence directly or indirectly in getting me on the road to being an Ideal Woman:

My Heavenly Mother, Blessed Virgin Mary

My earthly mother, Grace Egbejimba

My mother-in-law, Theresa Nnanabu, who has gone to be with the Lord

ACKNOWLEDGMENTS

"Now to Him who is able to do immeasurably more than all we ask or imagine according to His power that is at work within us, to Him be glory in the church and in Christ Jesus throughout all generations, for ever and ever! Amen."

Ephesians 3:20–21

And as always, to the love of my life, my best friend, my sweetheart, my husband, Jerry, thank you, thank you. Thank you for your love, support, prayers, belief in me, patience, and understanding with me during all those long nights I stayed awake writing this book. Thank you also for performing all the computer duties and for editing my manuscript. Honey, you know that next to God, you are closest in my life. I am deeply and joyfully in love with you.

Jerry, you are the best, the wind beneath my wings! I love you.

Thank you!

To my three beautiful children, Somutoo, Chubie, and Ihuoma, thank you for taking over the cooking, groceries, laundry, and other errands while I disappeared upstairs working on this book. You three are the "salt," the flavor in my life. Mommy loves you.

I will never be able to adequately thank The Very Rev. Jim Northrop, my spiritual director, for his continued spiritual guidance, prayer, suggestions, and insights.

Father Jim, "May He who started the anointed and good work in you, continue to watch over you and see to its glorious completion in Jesus name. Amen!" (cf Philippians 1:6)

Finally, but not least, my special thanks to Mrs. Virginia King, for believing in the importance of this project when I approached her with the tremendous task of writing the foreword to this book. Virginia, thank you immensely for saying yes to this project, but most importantly, thank you for saying yes to God. You are truly an anointed handmaid of the Lord, an ideal woman!

PREFACE

As a young unmarried person, I read Proverbs 31 very often and dreamed of what it would be like to be the Ideal Wife and Mother. All through my twenty-one years of marriage, the Proverbs 31 woman has challenged me and continues to challenge me daily to use my God-given talents in as many areas as possible as a wife and mother. I strive daily to be the best wife and mother I can be, doing all and everything I do to bring glory and honor to God. I am not where God wants me to be yet. I am still a "work in progress," but I am confident that He who began a good work in me will carry it on to completion until the day of Christ Jesus (cf. Philippians 1:6).

Now let's talk, heart-to-heart, person to person, tête-à-tête. I know that God never wastes anything; I tell my children that I have come to believe that one of God's mottos might be "Waste not, want not." There is a message for every woman in Proverbs 31. That passage in the Bible was not written just because! Of course, nobody could perform all the functions mentioned in this passage in one day, but at the same time, let us prayerfully pay attention to what God is saying to us women in this day and age in contrast to what our secular humanistic society is telling us to do: "Whatever, wherever, whenever (no holds barred)…If it feels good to you, do it."

Again, let me emphasize that there is a message for every woman, young or old, in Proverbs 31. It does not matter if you are single, married, divorced, or widowed. It does not even matter if you do or do not have children. God has given women a model, and if we are willing to be open to have the opportunity to try our very best, we will be amazed at what God can and will do in and with our lives. I will be the first woman to tell you that I don't personally appreciate the fact that this ideal woman makes her own clothes (verse 22), because I don't know how to sew. But even at that, I am still willing to hang out with this woman to learn from her. I don't compare myself with her because I cannot. Psalm 139 tells me that I am unique; I am one of a kind. And you—yes, you—are also very unique, wonderfully and fearfully made by God in your mother's womb. You are an original, not an imitation.

Do you realize that God is such a master at what He does that He makes no two raindrops, no two birthmarks, and no two women alike? So relax. Don't get your tentacles out, don't get defensive; we are not trying to compare ourselves with this, our new friend. We are only trying to learn from her.

She is our role model. You see, if you do not know what your destination is, you won't know when you get there. Proverbs 31 woman is our mirror. Nobody is perfect. I do understand that some of us have had our shares of brokenness and hurts in life. Some of us have been through some bad marriages and abusive relationships. Some of us have dotted all the "i's" and crossed all the "t's" and still ended up with unruly children. Yet God still loves us exactly where we are.

My sister, forward-thinking and open-minded people position themselves to succeed. I am praying for you to have the openness to learn new ideas as you read this book. All the suggestions in this book are ideas that have worked for me. There are lots of other ways in which our sovereign God, in His redemptive power, uses to touch lives. It does not matter how messed up your life has been or is right now. God is loving you right now, just as you are. His mercy is bigger than your mess. He can turn your mess into a message if you let Him. He did it for the Samaritan woman at the well in John 4. The Samaritan woman had at least two things against her: her mixed ethnic lineage and her very unacceptable marital situation. But Jesus still reached out to her, to show that each of us is loved no matter what our story is. Always remember, no mess is beyond God's touch of grace. God wants you to grow from passivity to being active, from whining to winning, and from a victim's mentality to a victor's attitude.

The fact that you are reading this book at such a time as this is not a coincidence. Remember, God ordained all the days of your life from the start, and He has specific plans for you. This new friend in Proverbs 31 has her life centered in God, and because of that she has a self-image based on the values of God. The only one who can give you a real sense of value is God. So, first things come first, my dear friend. Is your life centered in God? Only you can answer that question for yourself. Just in case you have not put God first in your life, this is your time, this is your day. Just do it. Do not let anything or anyone stop you from putting God first in your life right now. I always ask women, "Who is in charge of your life? Who is your CEO, your commander in chief?" It better be God. He must be first. Your life must be centered in Him. When you surrender your entire life to God, your love for Him will make you want to honor Him in all that you do, say, or think everyday of your life—24/7.

Life is all about choice, not chance. Make a decision today to be in God's perfect will and not only in His permissive will. Your decision will determine your destiny. Even God does not manipulate your destiny. He gives you a choice. Decide today to put Him first in all areas and aspects of your life. He will honor your faithfulness and give you the grace you need to be who He created you to be. God's grace is the accomplisher of His purpose. He says, "My grace is sufficient for you" (2 Corinthians 12:9a).

This book is about empowerment. It is a journey of discovery of how you, as a woman, are empowered to know who you really are and who you really belong to. It is most gratifying to know that you are the daughter of the King of kings. You are a princess! And you are loved by your Father beyond your wildest imagination. Read and enjoy!

Remain blessed in His love and grace. Amen!

Stella Nnanabu

INTRODUCTION

By
REVEREND JIM NORTHROP,

SPIRITUAL DIRECTOR,
WESTERN WASHINGTON CATHOLIC
CHARISMATIC RENEWAL

We are living in difficult times. I frequently find myself trying to encourage the people I have been called to serve to stay on the narrow path and keep their eyes fixed on Jesus Christ (c.f. Hebrews 12:2). So many people start off with a sure footing but slip and fall and are lured away by the temptations of the world and the evil one. This is certainly the case with marriages. We are living in a world of great uncertainty, and people are trying to find a sense of purpose and meaning in their lives. I am growing daily in my love and understanding of our Lord's teaching about the Parable of the Sower (cf. Matthew). It is so important that we cultivate fertile ground to allow the seed of new life given to us by Jesus to grow so that we can bear true fruits of righteousness and embrace our call to holiness.

One thing I always find refreshing is that when the Holy Spirit falls upon someone, the person is empowered to reclaim the standard and call to holiness rather than sit back and complain about how wrong everything is. I believe the Holy Spirit makes us positive, pro-active, and effective in bearing witness to the new life Jesus has won for us. We have Good News! Scripture reminds us that we are called to "overcome evil with good" (Romans 12:21).

Stella Nnanabu's *You–An Ideal Woman* provides us with a beautiful picture of what constitutes the ideal woman. Her writing is straightforward, practical, and effective. She draws upon her own experiences and how she has found great joy in striving to embrace the call God has given her. We need more holy women in our church today who trust in the Lord with all their heart and understand the importance of being a good model and an effective witness for Christ.

May you find great encouragement in this book, and may all of us cherish the gift of godly women and affirm our call to build up the Body of Christ through our own striving not to be conformed to the thinking of this world but to be transformed by the renewal of our mind.

FOREWORD
By
MRS. VIRGINIA KING

EXECUTIVE DIRECTOR,
WESTERN WASHINGTON CATHOLIC
CHARISMATIC RENEWA

As Christian women, we are on a journey to grow into maturity, to become all that God created us to be. This includes, above all, learning to love God with all our mind, heart, soul, strength, and will, and loving others as Jesus has loved us. This is a call for us to continue to grow in holiness day by day.

In speaking about the "universal call to holiness," Pope John Paul II speaks first of holiness as a gift from God. He then says,

> "But the gift in turn becomes a task, which must shape the whole of Christian life: 'This is the will of God, your sanctification' (1 Thessalonians 4:3). It is a duty which concerns not only certain Christians: 'All the Christian faithful, of whatever state or rank, are called to the fullness of the Christian life and to the perfection of charity.'"[1]

I always think of this quote when I think about striving for an ideal in the Christian life. Whatever ways we come close to the ideal and whatever good we achieve is a gift from God, "but the gift in turn becomes a task."

In this book, Stella Nnanabu exhorts us to strive for a particular ideal, that of being an ideal woman according to the description in Proverbs 31:10–31. And though the grace to achieve this ideal is totally a gift from God, "the gift in turn becomes a task."

It would be easy to read this Scripture and quickly decide that it doesn't apply to us today. This ideal wife of Proverbs 31 is obviously wealthy, talented, and well educated. And she lived in a time with many fewer distractions. But Stella has drawn out of this Scripture some general principles that apply not only to the ideal "wife" but beyond that to every woman, married or not.

As I read this book, I became aware that Stella herself has benefited from many "ideal" women and men in her own life, including her parents, husband, and children. She approaches this Scripture from her own experience as a wife, mother, sister, friend, and mentor. As she shares examples from her own life, you might begin to think that she has an unfair advantage—your own background might be very different and your own experience may include coming from a dysfunctional family or the pain of a broken marriage.

Yet, regardless of our background, there is something for each of us to learn from Proverbs 31. "All scripture is inspired by God and is useful for teaching… and for training in righteousness so that everyone who belongs to God may be proficient, equipped for every good work" (2 Timothy 3:16–17). Stella exhorts us to allow the example of the "ideal wife" to help us to grow, to train us up in righteousness in order that we might attain the high standard of holiness to which we are called.

My own journey of trying to mature in my various relationships as a wife, mother, daughter, sister, friend, and mentor is long and unfinished. I have at least as many failures as I do successes. But the most important thing I have learned along the way is that this is all about grace. It is about relying on God for the help we need. One of Stella's key concepts and mottos is LPP: Love, Patience, and Prayer. If you learn nothing else in reading this book, it is worth remembering LPP.

Chapter by chapter, this book is like meeting with Stella over coffee, having a chat with a friend who really cares about you and wants to help you grow in holiness. Stella helps us to set the bar high, to strive for perfection, and to rejoice in every small bit of progress we make. Seeking maturity in the grace of God means that we are not trapped by our circumstances but rather that we are able to rise above them in freedom. We have the freedom and ability, by the grace of God, to change our ways of thinking and acting.

One warning though, don't try to incorporate all of Stella's suggestions at the same time! I think that would be overwhelming. As with all efforts to grow in maturity, it's wise to make one change at a time and to make it a permanent part of your life. For example, if you don't already have a strong habit of daily personal prayer, the first chapter of this book is an important first step in your growth in maturity. Develop a strong prayer life. Without this, none of the rest will make sense, nor will it be possible.

In the preface, Stella talks about knowing who we are in God. This is so critical. Our identity comes first from being beloved children of God. Once we realize this truth deep in our own being, then we can begin to spread this good news to others. This is a message that not only women need to hear but men need to hear too. We need to be able to convey this to our parents (if they are still with us), to our spouses, our siblings, our children, and our friends.

One of the key concepts in this book revolves around the topic of being countercultural. Stella asks very pointed questions that really make you think. If you have children, part of being countercultural involves taking responsibility for your children, not relinquishing responsibility to their teachers or to anyone else. But even if you don't have children of your own, you can make a difference by being a countercultural model of Christian life to the young people you know.

Another key concept follows this one, that of mentoring others in the ways of the Lord. As women, we have a lot to teach each other and are able to likewise learn from one another. Our styles of communication may vary, but it is deep inside of us to want to nurture others and help one another succeed in life, in faith, in marriage, and in mothering. This is exactly what Stella has done through this book.

Remember, we are all a work in progress. As the saying goes, "Please be patient, God is not finished with me yet." We need to be patient with ourselves and ask others to be patient with us as we grow to maturity in Jesus, our Lord. As we learn from the ideal wife of Proverbs 31, step by step we will be learning to love God with all our mind, heart, soul, strength, and will, and to love others as Jesus has loved us.

PROVERBS

31:10–31

A capable wife who can find?
 She is far more precious than jewels.
The heart of her husband trusts in her,
 and he will have no lack of gain.
She does him good, and not harm,
 all the days of her life.
She seeks wool and flax,
 and works with willing hands.
She is like the ships of the merchant,

she brings her food from far away.
She rises while it is still night
 and provides food for her household
 and tasks for her servant-girls.
She considers a field and buys it;
 with the fruit of her hands she plants a vineyard.
She girds herself with strength,
 and makes her arms strong.
She perceives that her merchandise is profitable.
 Her lamp does not go out at night.
She puts her hands to the distaff,
 and her hands hold the spindle.
She opens her hand to the poor,
 and reaches out her hands to the needy.
She is not afraid for her household when it snows,
 for all her household are clothed in crimson.
She makes herself coverings;
 her clothing is fine linen and purple.
Her husband is known in the city gates,
 taking his seat among the elders of the land.
She makes linen garments and sells them;

she supplies the merchant with sashes.
Strength and dignity are her clothing,
  and she laughs at the time to come.
She opens her mouth with wisdom,
  and the teaching of kindness is on her tongue.
She looks well to the ways of her household,
  and does not eat the bread of idleness.
Her children rise up and call her happy;
  her husband too, and he praises her:
"Many women have done excellently,
  but you surpass them all."
Charm is deceitful, and beauty is vain,
  but a woman who fears the Lord is to be praised.
Give her a share in the fruit of her hands,
  and let her works praise her in the city gates.

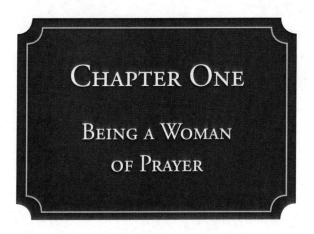

CHAPTER ONE

BEING A WOMAN OF PRAYER

"*C*harm is deceitful, and beauty is vain, but a woman who fears the lord is to be praised."

Proverbs 31:30

When you read everything about this ideal friend of ours, you could tell that the secret behind her success in every aspect of her life is her relationship with her God. She "fears the Lord" (verse 30). Fear here is a reverential type of fear that makes her approach God with proper respect for His holiness. "The fear of the Lord is the beginning of wisdom, and the knowledge of the Holy one is insight" (Proverbs 9:10). With this proper respect for God's holiness in mind, we approach God only on His terms, in the manner He prescribes, being constantly aware of the fact that the privilege of approaching God is itself a gift of God's grace, a gift that must not be taken lightly.

This ideal woman of Proverbs 31 does not take this gracious gift of God lightly. She took time out of her busy schedule to spend some quality time daily studying and learning more about this Holy God. How do I know this? Verse 15 tells me that she gets up very early in the morning before dawn, "while it is still night." Do you wonder why? I imagine that this is her "Quiet Time," quiet time alone with her God in praise and worship, in prayer, in Bible study, and in dedicating her whole day to her God. No wonder she is a wise woman who knows very well that unless her life is spiritually well grounded and centered in God, she cannot possibly be a wife of noble character, an excellent homemaker, a successful businesswoman, and a very good ambassador for Christ. I never want to meet with anybody on any given day without meeting with my God first. He is my commander in chief.

When my children were little, I woke up at five a.m. for my quiet time. Now that they are older, I wake up at six a.m. for my one-hour quiet time with the Lord. Prayer is the only thing that gives us access into the presence of the Father. For me, on weekends, I spend over an hour in prayer; sometimes I am gone for two hours. "Doing what?" you ask. I always start off with praise and worship. Praise and worship are the best part of my prayer time because praise and worship put me in God's lap. Talk about heaven on earth … you cannot even begin to imagine what it feels like to be in the throne room of your Father, the King of all kings, and sitting on His lap. After praise and worship, I read my Bible. Then comes another huge part of my prayer time—intercessory prayers. My husband, Jerry, and I have an intercessory prayer ministry, and we have a very long list of people, places, events, petitions, requests, heart desires, dreams, visions, politicians, nations, pastors, and other ministries to pray for. Then I spend some time in silence to allow my spirit to hear what God is saying to me. At the end, I pray over my schedule for the day. If I perceive a tough day at work, I pray for wisdom to do or say the right thing to the right person at the right time.

Just recently, I started doing a type of contemplative prayer called centering prayer, and I love it. I keep a prayer journal too. I just cannot function without my quiet time, even when I am on vacation. As I already mentioned, I never want to meet with anybody, any day, without meeting with my God first—never! The quiet time gives me the opportunity to be fed spiritually. It is time for my spiritual breakfast, and you know that breakfast is the most important meal of the day. Having been fed, I am equipped to spiritually nourish my family. I pray that all of you beautiful women are feeding your family a balanced diet to nourish both the soul and the body. Although I read my Bible every morning, I study my Bible in more depth a couple nights a week.

How to Have a Daily Prayer Time

Since you have decided to make God the center of your life, spending time daily with God will help keep Him there—at the center of your life. This is what "Quiet Time" is all about. I believe and I know that Quiet Time is the secret of a Christian's daily life and that Christians who constantly keep their appointments with God daily grow spiritually:

1. The first thing to do is to select a time that fits your personal schedule. Most people prefer the morning hours, but the morning hours may not fit into everybody's schedule. The most important thing here is to set aside a time that you will keep every single day come rain or shine.

2. Select a place where you will be alone with God the entire time. Since we are all very unique individuals, my advice is to be yourself; let the Holy Spirit lead and guide you. The practical aspect of Quiet Time is not a one size fits all. I know some people who prefer to have their own Quiet Time after taking a shower and their morning cup of coffee or tea because that is the way for them to be awake and alert. I know some women who wait to have their Quiet Time after dropping off the children at school. Still some women drive out to a lonely place during their lunch hour and sit in their car to meet with God. I have mine first thing in the morning after brushing my teeth (very important to me), in my pajamas, with my hair curlers. My sister Julia has a prayer room in her house where she has her Quiet Time. God will lead you to your spot, to your "prayer closet" (Matthew 6:6).

3. Although I sit during my Quiet Time, some people, like my husband, prefer to kneel by their bedside. Again, be yourself; there is no

hard-and-fast rule about the position to take. If you are sleepy or fatigued, you can walk and pray out loud. I know people can walk and sleep, but you cannot walk, pray, and sleep at the same time. Do whatever helps you to concentrate and have quality time with your God. There is something helpful about having your Quiet Time at the same time and place each day if possible. It has something to do with the human mind and psyche. Mothers, it's just like having a bedtime routine for our little ones. You know how that gets them ready for bed.

4. Be sure to have all the materials you need ready to go: your Bible, your prayer books, your notebook or prayer journal, pen or pencil, your daily Bible reading guide (if you use any), etc. Some people like some music for praise and worship, and they have their CD player ready to go. I have a friend who plays her guitar, singing praises to God during her Quiet Time. Try to personalize your Quiet Time to avoid being in a rut.

5. Your primary focus should be on God, the person you are meeting with, and not really on the habit itself. Think about a daily appointment with the president of your country. Aha! I see your eyes lighting up. Now, think again; a daily appointment with the President of all presidents, the King of all kings, the Lord of all lords, the Omnipotent, Omnipresent, Omniscient Creator who spoke this world into existence, the Immutable God, the Almighty God, the Most High God, the Everlasting God, the Alpha, the Omega, the Beginning, the End, the Jehovah Jireh, the Jehovah Nissi, the Jehovah Rophi, the Jehovah Elshaddai, the Jehovah Shammah, the Jehovah Yékaddia, the Jehovah Shalom, the Jehovah Zidkenu, the Jehovah Roi, Elohim, Adonai, El Elyon... Get it? How many times in your lifetime do you get to meet with the president of your country? Close to zero. But God, in His divine mercy, created us with the ability to fellowship with Him. What an enormous gift! What an awesome grace! What a benevolent favor! This

is the basic principle of the Quiet Time—fellowship with the lover of your soul. God desires your daily fellowship with Him. It is important to Him too, and He looks forward to it. Lovers like to be together. So look forward to fellowshipping with your God every day. Do it out of love for your Lover and not out of habit.

6. Persistence with your Quiet Time will gradually lead to consistency. Consistency is the goal rather than the length of time spent. The length of time spent does not really matter that much as long as you are having a quality Quiet Time every day. Put in layman's terms, having a quality Quiet Time every day for even twenty to thirty minutes is far better than having an hour of Quiet Time every other day or every two days. Just like your mother always told you, "Don't skip meals," and that was just about feeding your physical body. Why would you want to skip meals in regards to nourishment for your soul? No wonder there are so many "spiritual anorexics" running around. Their poor souls

are being starved to death. Take one day at a time if this is new to you and plan on consistency.

7. Developing new habits, changing, or breaking old habits is just not easy. Carefully and zealously guard your Quiet Time, because Satan will personally do everything in his power to interrupt, prevent, and oppose your spending time in fellowship with God. Satan knows the benefits of Quiet Time more than most Christians. One of the benefits of daily Quiet Time is that you go from just knowing about God to coming to know God. There is a big difference in knowing about God and coming to know God. Many Christians know about God all right but have not taken the time to come to know God. Believing is no longer enough; we have got to get to the next level of coming to know God. The daily Quiet Time gives you that wonderful opportunity to spend time one-on-one personally, not corporately with God. Obviously, Satan does not want you to come to know God. *Hello!* Again, Satan will personally do every-

thing in his power to interrupt, prevent, and oppose your Quiet Time. He will consistently send time-stealers your way. Be persistent. It will be a daily battle. If Satan doesn't want to give up, why do you want to give up? Be persistent. Dig in your high heels, my dear ladies, and let's make the devil so mad that he can get out of the planet for good.

Below is an order I have used for over thirty years (I can't believe I am that young!) for my Quiet Time. We cannot script everything in our lives, so it's okay to be flexible to the move of the Holy Spirit. You don't want your Quiet Time to be mechanical or rigid. Here we go …

Adoration

Praise God for His presents and worship Him for His presence. In layman's (oops, laywoman's) terms, praise God for what He does and worship Him for who He is. Nothing fancy here. You don't have to praise and worship God in Old King James English or in eloquent Victorian English (O Thou Majestic King!). Do you know that God can speak and understand French, Latin, Spanish, Swahili, Tagalog, Japanese, Igbo, Korean, Chinese, Yoruba, Vietnamese, Hausa, German, Portuguese, Italian, Arabic, Indian, Russian, Hawaiian, Dutch, etc.? If you are gifted in the charismatic gift of tongues, do use it often to praise and worship God.

Confession

Start with the examination of yourself. I like the fact that Confession follows Adoration. The Holy Spirit of God has a way of helping us sort through ourselves. Acknowledge your sins and faults, repent of them, confess them, and ask God for forgiveness. Caution: A note of warning for those of us who are Catholics. This does not take the place of the sacrament of Reconciliation. Rather, it is an excellent preparation for making a good Sacramental confession.

Bible Reading

Please, if you don't have a Bible, get one today! Get yourself a daily Bible reading guide too. Have a plan. I have read the Bible in the past years by chapters and by books. Now, I am into reading the Bible by subjects. The Bible does not *contain* the Word of God; the Bible *is* the Word of God, so make it your constant guide and companion in life. You need to know the Word (the Bible) for yourself.

Thanksgiving

This is the time to thank God for anything and everything in your life. I mean the big miracles and the little miracles. Thank God in advance for answers to your petitions, requests, intercessions, and prayers. Thank God in your trials, temptations, mountain-tops, storms, deserts, and valleys. You know why you should thank God in all your circumstances? Because He said so, "Give thanks in all circumstances, for this is the will of God in Christ Jesus for you" (1 Thessalonians 5:18). God's will is that we thank Him *in* all circumstances, not *for* all circumstances, because our circumstances do change, but our Almighty God never changes.

Our God is the unchangeable Changer. So we learn to be thankful to the sovereign God regardless of the external conflicts in our lives, regardless of whether we are at the mountaintop or at the valley of death. We learn to be continuously aware of the faithfulness and goodness of our God who is the same, yesterday, today, and forever (Hebrews 13:8). This is how we remain in that inner peace that only God can give in times of crisis; that peace of God that is not the absence of external crisis but the power of internal security; that peace that makes people gossip about your demeanor when you are in the middle of a storm and they expect you to be a complete basketcase and you are not.

Supplication

This includes intercession and petition. Intercession is a prayer presenting the needs of others to God. There is power in intercessory prayers. Jerry and I have been partners in our intercessory prayer ministry for over ten years, and believe me when I tell you that we have seen God move mountains (literally). Do you know that you have the power to change hearts on your knees? Prayer is one of the greatest gifts you can give or receive. More than ever, we need more men and women going on their knees and moving the hands of God in our nations, in our churches, in our families, in our schools, in our neighborhoods, in our hospitals, in our prisons, in our offices, in our media, in our cities, in our towns, in our villages, and in the world today.

Petition is a prayer presenting your own needs to God. I don't know about you, but my list is a very long one. But guess what? My very long list doesn't overwhelm my God. There is nothing too insignificant to ask God for. I have been known to ask God for a particular color of shoe to go with a particular outfit. There is nothing too big to ask God for. I have asked God to make me a millionaire, and this is not a joke. The point I am trying to make is that nothing is too big or too small to ask God for, because He is able to do far more than all we ask or think to ask (Ephesians 3:20). About my millionaire status, what we discern God is asking my husband and I to do in our ministry, to spread the gospel, requires thousands of dollars. When God begins to dream through you, you need money for those dreams to come through.

Silence

This is the time to listen to God. Silence is a blessed gift needed terribly in today's world. We have almost completely lost this wonderful art today. Simply sit, close your eyes, and listen. It helps to write down whatever words, thoughts, and pictures come into your mind. Sometimes the words, the thoughts, or the pictures won't make sense to you right away, and this is why I suggest that you write them down and just wait. With time you will get some clarity, some confirmation, some meaning to what God is trying to communicate to you. Just like two lovers together do not need to use words to express their love for each other, God may also decide to be silent in your silence.

Here is a brief explanation of the names of God used in this chapter:

Jehovah Jireh–The Lord Who Provides (Genesis 22:14)

Jehovah Nissi–The Lord Our Banner (Exodus 17:15)

Jehovah Rophi–The Lord Who Heals (Exodus 15:26)

Jehovah Elshaddai–God Almighty (Exodus 6:3)

Jehovah Shammah–The Lord at Hand (Ezekiel 48:35)

Jehovah Yekaddia–The Lord Who Sanctifies (Exodus 31:13)

Jehovah Zidkenu–The Lord Our Righteousness (Jeremiah 23:6)

Jehovah Shalom–The Lord Our Peace (Judges 6:24)

El Elyon–The Lord Who Owns, God Most High (Genesis 14:22)

Jehovah Roi–The Lord Our Shepherd (Psalm 23:1)

Elohim–The Lord Who Creates (Genesis 2:4)

Adonai–The Lord Our Master, Our Sovereign Lord (Genesis 15:2)

Chapter Two

Being a Wife of Noble Character

"A capable wife who can find? She is far more precious than jewels. The heart of her husband trusts in her, and he will have no lack of gain. She does him good, and not harm, all the days of her life."

Proverbs 31:10–12

My wonderful husband, Jerry, is a cool, relaxed, levelheaded man. Nothing bothers him. His favorite

saying when we are trying to figure out how to solve
a problem is, "We will see when the time comes."
Another one of his favorite sayings when I am trying to think, reason things out, analyze every minute detail, is this, "C, relax, God will take care of it."
And here I am hanging from the ceiling, looking at
my husband with disdain, wondering whether he is
silly and trying to figure out what he really means by,
"Relax." I am very strict, firm, taut, detailed, analyti-
cal, and nitpicky. Did I say I am bossy too?! I spent
my first few years of marriage trying to change Jerry.
The more I tried to change him, the more he made
me mad, because to me, he was just not getting it. I
nagged, screamed, threw fits, but Jerry kept his cool.
I got mad at him because he was peaceful when I
was busy running around trying to think out and
reason out everything, sweating both the small and
big stuff. Contrary to what I am now, I didn't use to
be this little, nice, soft, and sweet wife. I was always
in a hurry, always stressed out.

I have had my own share of struggles too. I have struggled with being a submissive wife for so many years. Finally, God made it clear to me that the only way He would use me in ministry was if I learned to submit to the authority of my husband. Submission in a Christian family is mutual and very important to the life of the family. Our God has ordained order rather than disorder. He recognizes the need to live together in harmony. This mutual submission is based on our Christian faith, and it understands authority as servanthood. Jesus is a very good example of the servant role of leadership. Submission is a word frowned at today by most women, but it is a Christian attitude that allows a wife to voluntarily yield in love to the headship of her husband.

One morning, I heard God loud and clear during my quiet time, "Stella, stop trying to change your husband, Jerry. Learn to be a wife of noble character." I think I was actually praying for Jerry to change when God spoke to me. Proverbs 27:12 says, "The prudent see danger and take refuge, but the simple keep going and suffer for it." I saw danger, I listened to God, and I took refuge in Proverbs 31:10–31. This is how I started hanging out with the Proverbs 31 woman. *Wow!* She is the best! I have learned a lot from her. I learned to be flexible. I learned to be an encourager and to look for the good in my husband. Most importantly, I learned to keep my mouth shut when I do not have anything nice to say. This is still a tough one for me.

What makes one a wife of noble character?

Let's see how the dictionary explains the words "noble" and "prudent."

noble - having or showing qualities of high moral character, as courage, generosity, honor.

prudent - wise in practical matters; careful in regards to one's own interests; careful about one's conduct.

Get it? God wants us to be wise, courageous, generous, of high moral character, and careful about our conduct. He wants us to be women of honor. He wants us to be wise and to put our wisdom into action in choosing practical and constructive ways to live and work.

Another very important quality of this, our new friend, is that she is trustworthy. Talk about a needed quality in today's marriages—the "T" word. My pastor, Father Tom, in one of his talks to married couples at the Lovers' Celebration Mass, said, "Trust is the oil of relationships. Without trust there is friction and heat, because that is the nature of human relationship." Without trust, there can be no commitment in marriage. Could this have anything to do with the high divorce rate in our society today? The goal here is family success. Without trust and commitment, there will not be the respect and honor needed for family success. Satan, being very strategic in his attacks, has decided to go after our families. When we come together as families, the devil will have to run. That's why the devil does not want families to get together and stay together. Think about this. Every community is a family of families. Our church community is a family of families. Our school community is a family of families. Even our work community is a family of families.

I pray to the good Lord every day to give me the grace to be trustworthy to my husband, so that he can have full confidence in me and "have no lack of gain" (verse 11). What does it mean for a husband to "have no lack of gain"? I went to God for an insight on this, and what I found out touched me greatly. In the New International Version translation, it says he will "lack nothing of value." When a husband has full (not partial) confidence in his wife, he feels very secure in himself. A secure man is a confident man. A confident man is very comfortable under his skin, even to the point of not being afraid to admit that he is not perfect. Isn't this an awesome, awesome virtue to see in our husbands? And hopefully, eventually we see them in our sons.

This is a man who is comfortable and humble enough to say, "I am sorry, I was wrong." A secure, confident, and humble man will not have the need to be chauvinistic or opinionated to prove that he is always right. Even when he is right, true humility will still make him say, "I think I am right, I believe I am right, but I could be wrong." Now check this out, this happy, humble, secure, and confident husband turns around to praise his wife (verse 28). Do you see the chain reaction and the wonderful results? The wife takes a relational risk and takes the first step to be trustworthy; the husband in return feels secure, confident, humble, happy, and praises the wife. The wife is happy, the husband is happy, and "her children rise up and call her happy" (verse 28). This is a win-win situation because everyone in the family is happy. I tell you, God knows what He is doing, if only we will listen to Him and obey Him.

This wife of noble character also "does her husband good, not harm, all the days of her life" (verse 12), not some days of the month. Yeep! You read my mind... PMS is not an excuse anymore. Believe me when I say that God is a fixer-upper. He is in the business of rebuilding, remodeling, restoring, repairing, recovering, refacing, refreshing, replenishing, and redeeming–(buying back... sounds like a real estate agent to me). I have come a very, very long way. I used to announce to my wonderful husband and to my beautiful children that time of the month when I am a Potential Murder Suspect (PMS). I look back at those years and I thank God for being an excellent real estate agent—the best, as a matter of fact.

I have learned to do good and not harm to my wonderful husband all the days of the month. Jerry is a homebody and likes a clean house, good food, and good sex (I cannot believe I just said that!). He likes to laugh, and we are constantly cracking jokes and poking fun at each other. Making laughter an important part of our friendship has helped us grow closer to each other. When he goes out of town, I sneak funny pictures of me and the children into his suitcase so he can find them later on in his trip and laugh. Laughter, and I mean real, deep down belly laughter, does wonders. It's a very healthy emotional exercise given to us by God to help us release, relieve, and relax. Learn to laugh at each other and with each other. It does your body good. I am Jerry's best friend and he is my best friend. He likes to look sharp, so I dress him up good. Jerry does not like to be talked down to or yelled at... so I am still working on this!

Let me share one thing we have done as a married couple of twenty-one years. We go out on a date once every month. Usually, we start with dinner, then we go to a movie or dancing. When our third child goes off to college, we will increase the frequency of our dates to once a week. I cannot begin to imagine what our marriage would have been like without our monthly dates these past twenty-one years. With full-time careers, three very busy children, and a ministry, we need time to reconnect and recharge our romance. This is a big romantic event every month for both of us. We look forward to it, and we dress up good for it too. I always tell people, including my own children, that the right place for dating is after marriage. I will go into more detail in the next chapter.

Men prefer respect to affection, unlike women. I have learned to focus more on Jerry's good qualities and compliment him more. There was a month that my cleaning lady went to visit her sick mother in California, and my awesome husband decided to take a weekend job of cleaning the house. I leave very early on Saturday mornings to take my daughter to her ballet, jazz, and modern dance classes. By the time we got home at noon, the whole house was sparkling clean. One Saturday, I went into the bathroom and noticed some dried water spots on the bathroom mirror, and I started murmuring to myself while I was using the bathroom. I heard it again, loud and clear, "Stella, shut up and be grateful for what you have." I looked up to God and said, "Sorry." I went to my husband and thanked him for doing such an exceptional job of cleaning, dusting, mopping, vacuuming, and even wiping down the bathroom mirrors. He was very happy!

There is something about being appreciated. I have never seen a person who does not appreciate being appreciated. Men love to be praised and complimented. Could you have even imagined what could have happened if I had busted out of the bathroom whining about him forgetting to wipe down the bathroom mirror? The rest of the day would have been ruined for him and for me. It is amazing the positive changes we can see in our husbands when we take the initiative to do good and not harm to them.

Verse 26 tells us that this new friend "opens her mouth with wisdom." The tongue! The *tongue! The tongue!* I love this woman, and she is so very worthy of my emulation. I don't know about you, but I can be the sweetest person in this world outside my home, but when my husband or my children rub me the wrong way... oh my goodness! My tongue goes out of control. Oh yes, I told you, I am not a saint. I am learning to open "my mouth with wisdom," especially when I am upset with my wonderful husband and my beautiful children. The Holy Spirit kept convicting me over and over about my tongue, and I eventually went to my spiritual director, who asked me to go home and study the book of James. I did, and I thank God for His grace in this area.

Ladies, wives, let's learn to open our mouths with wisdom. Do not be rude or sarcastic, because that will keep you from being who God wants you to be. Be more understanding and not demanding, especially if you have a bossy tone of voice like mine. If you want to be persuasive, make your words more pleasurable. There is power of life and death in the tongue. So let our pledge be: "Let the words of my mouth and the meditation of my heart be acceptable to you, O Lord my rock and my redeemer" (Psalm 19:14).

Some of you nice women reading this book might be thinking, *So what does my husband get to do if I am the one doing all these things?* or, *What if I have been doing all these things for a zillion years and my husband is still not being nice to me?* These are very good questions, very true-to-life questions and situations. I am not trying to let the husbands off the hook here. Of course not! And I am not claiming to have all the answers. All these suggestions are ideas that have worked for me. They may or may not work for you, as every marriage is different and unique too.

Marriage is a two-way street, but contrary to the popular notion, it is not always 50/50 or 100/100. Let's look at the traffic on Interstate-5 (I-5) on a particular day. Sometimes, especially during the morning rush hours, traffic is more going north on I-5, from Tacoma to Seattle. And during the late afternoon rush hours, traffic is more going South on I-5, from Seattle to Tacoma. Traffic may be 50/50 on I-5 during the noontime. This is how marriage is. As I continue to study God's Word and grow spiritually, I have come to learn that God wants us women to be good examples in our homes, not only to our husbands, but also to our children and others around us. Be the first to step out in love and obedience to God to do what is right, even if no one else is doing so. Your husband and children are reading the gospel when they look at you. What are they reading? Are you living out the principles and precepts of God?

Start taking initiatives to sow the right seeds of love, patience, and prayers in your family, even when it looks like nobody really cares. God cares, and He will reward you in His own time. "So let us not grow weary in doing what is right, for we will reap at harvest time, if we do not give up" (Galatians 6:9). Love, Patience, and Prayers (LPP) work wonders and can be applied to all kinds of situation. LPP has worked for me in some difficult and different situations. Onward, Christian women ... let us desire to make a mark for God in all that we do and say, so help us God. Amen!

Let's review the life of Saint Monica, the mother of Saint Augustine. Saint Monica was a good example of a patient, loving woman of prayer. She was born in the year 352 in Tagaste, North Africa. Although she was a Christian by birth, she was given in marriage to a bad-tempered pagan man. Their home could not have been a very happy one, but Saint Monica remained very patient and loving. She prayed constantly for the conversion of her husband and lived an exemplary life of gentleness and kindness. A year before his death, Monica's husband converted and became a Christian. First Peter 3:1–2 says,

> Wives, in the same way, accept the authority of your husbands, so that, even if some of them do not obey the word, they may be won over without a word by their wives' conduct, when they see the purity and reverence of your lives.

Saint Monica had two sons and a daughter. The other son and the daughter were exemplary children. But Augustine was not. Augustine, though very brilliant, was also very worldly. His worldliness caused his mother a lot of anguish and pain. Saint

Monica again did not lose faith. She was very loving, patient, and prayerful. She constantly fasted, prayed, and wept on his behalf. God, in His faithfulness, answered her prayers, and her wayward son eventually converted and became a Christian.

CHAPTER THREE

BEING AN EXCELLENT HOMEMAKER

"She looks well to the ways of her household, and does not eat the bread of idleness."

Proverbs 31:27

This wife of noble character is also an excellent homemaker. She is very active at home and very organized. She is not lazy. Her work attitude is awesome; she actually "works with willing hands" (verse

13). Could she really be that enthusiastic about doing four loads of laundry at a time? Could she? How about changing nasty, stinky diapers? You mean she doesn't go around whining and complaining about being the "slave" around the house, picking up and cleaning up after everyone? She is actually able to see God in the ordinary, everyday, monotonous boredom of making and managing a home. I love this woman. I really, really want to emulate her, so help me God.

She is a diligent and watchful mom. My dear ladies, we should be our children's watchdog. We should develop a third eye in the back of our heads, a fourth and fifth on the sides of our heads, whatever it takes. Remember, our children are not ours but are on loan to us from God. We are raising ambassadors for Christ, future citizens of heaven. What are your children doing alone in their rooms and on their computers? Who are their friends and their friends' parents? If they are supposed to be somewhere, call to be sure they are there. You are not being a nosy mom; you are being an excellent mom who watches over the affairs of her household.

Mothers, it's okay to know a little bit more about your child's private life and room. Spring clean their rooms with them; make it a fun and relaxed thing. You are not trying to be "Inspector Gadget," but you are trying to know more about your child's private world. A knowledgeable mother is a better and wiser mom. Oh yes, I know all about the "Privacy Acts," but, at the same time, these are our children, and we are accountable to God for them. We cannot let the world dictate to us how to mother our children. Spring cleaning rooms with your children could be a fun Saturday thing to do. My children love it and look forward to it. It allows me to teach them how to organize their rooms, drawers, and closets. They love the fact that it is an opportunity to get rid of their old clothes, shoes, and hats for the poor and needy.

We are our children's primary teachers. Our children got used to the sound of our voices when they were in our wombs. Verse 26 tells us something very important about this, our new friend—she is an excellent teacher: "She opens her mouth with wisdom, and the teaching of kindness is on her tongue." The first classroom and, of course, the most important is the home. The significance of mothers and fathers as teachers in the house can never be over-emphasized. We teach our children both by words and by example. This ideal wife and mother takes it upon herself to train and nurture the minds of her children and maybe her neighbors' children.

Mothers, how well do you know your children? Have you taken the time to find out what makes each of your children unique? No two children are alike (thanks to God, the perfect Designer and Architect); even identical twins have their own individual uniqueness. Each child is matchless, one of a kind, with different personalities, likes, and dislikes. Because of this, we must desist treating our children in the same way. Take a look at what happens at the dinner table. One child cannot stand the sight of vegetables in any form imaginable—raw, cooked, steamed, sautéed, roasted, toasted, barbecued, or grilled (this is Chubie, my second son), while the other child can live on the five basic "junk" foods, like Twinkies, donuts, candy, potato chips, and ice cream (my daughter, Ihuoma). And then you have another child who loves a little bit of the good and bad (my Somutoo!). And you don't think God has a very fascinating sense of humor? I think so.

The point is this: We as homemakers must take the time to study our children to know what works and what doesn't work for each of them. Each child needs to be disciplined differently (Oh yeah!). Each child needs to be motivated differently (Zowee!). One child could be a good self and time manager, while the other child needs to be reminded at least ten millions times to do his/her homework. My dear, that's the way the "cookie crumbles." I thank God that I learned this early in the mothering years, or I would have ended up in jail or in a mental hospital (no kidding).

My two sons are twenty months apart and have very distinct personalities—totally night and day. Somutoo is very business-like, and Chubie is very laid back. One child will have me sign the parental release form a week ahead of the fieldtrip, and the other child will wake me up on the morning of the fieldtrip, hand me a pen, and have me sign the parental release form sleepy and in the dark. Get it? You see, I didn't have to mention any names, but I know you are a very smart woman of God and can figure things out easily.

Each child needs to be rewarded and complimented differently. The most important thing that we as mothers need to know is what brings pleasure to each and every member of our household. At Thanksgiving, I have to buy pecan pie for Jerry, apple pie for Somutoo, orange sherbet for Chubie, and ice cream for Ihuoma. Mothers, please take time to go out of your way to create a pleasant atmosphere in your home. Dedicate yourself to being the best homemaker you can possibly be, the most excellent homemaker God created you to be. Let your children yearn to come home. It does not matter what the four walls of the home look like. It could be an apartment, a condominium, a tent, a castle, a shack, a cottage, a tower, a thatched hut, a mud house, or a houseboat. It does not matter. Endeavor to make your children look forward to coming home to what I call "Mummy's little extras."

"North, south, east, or west, home is the best" is an old adage my mom always says. There is something special and fascinating about a loving home. Home for me is the place I can come back to (after looking at people's teeth all day) and be completely "naked." Not naked in the sense of nudity, but naked in the sense of being totally me, knowing that I am loved just the way I am. At the end of my workday, it is refreshing to know that I can go home, kick off my high heels, shut out the rest of the world, relax, and be Stella … yes, me! And I wish and want the same thing for my husband and children.

Most of our problems in this millennium stem from the fact that we have decided to spend more time and energy building and decorating our houses instead of "making" our homes. Most of the world's children today are lonely and "homeless" in their own homes. The only way to hit a "homerun" is to go back to the basics. Remember what the goal is again? The goal here is family success. Family success can only come from a home where there is love and understanding, where every member of the family feels loved, cared for, and respected, no matter what. Today's families shape and mold tomorrow's leaders—priests, nuns, pastors, mothers, fathers, politicians, musicians, doctors, nurses, attorneys, accountants, engineers, surveyors, carpenters, teachers, artists, architects, actors, photographers, entrepreneurs, scientists, and the list goes on.

We cannot have family success until every member of the family can come home at the end of their day, close the door, and feel free to be completely "naked." It should be okay for our children and our spouses to come home and feel free to express their sad, angry, tired, and hurting feelings. Whatever feelings have been brewing and bottled up all day can be completely emptied at home because we are surrounded by those who love and deeply care for us in a very special way. Now, if you have teenagers like I do, watch out (Yikes!). I have three of them, as I mentioned earlier. The moods they bring home at the end of the day can be hyper or withdrawn. To be very frank with you, I am having the best time of my mothering years now. I didn't know that being the mother of three teenagers could be this much fun! No, I am not kidding you, I really mean it. There's never a dull moment! If it is not drama on Broadway, it is a showdown on Hollywood Boulevard.

But I continue to thank God for His wisdom every day. Have I made mistakes? Of course, but God continues to teach me as I make myself open to His guidance, counseling, and directions. Daily I pray, "Lord, help me to will your will and to choose your choices for me today." One thing I learned about parenting from my own mom and dad is to "catch them young for Jesus." Another thing is goal setting. Goal setting does something magical for children, especially teenagers. When I was a teenager, my primary goal was to honor God and shine for Jesus in all that I did, and my second goal was to go to college and be a career woman someday. Thus, I miraculously escaped the rebelliousness of teenage years to the glory of God. When teenagers set goals for themselves, it helps them to direct and channel their energy to something specific. What extracurricular activities do your teens want to be involved in? What sports do they want to participate in? What ministry do they want to be involved in? Honestly speaking, I prefer my teenagers to have more than enough on their plates than to idle away surfing Web sites. My mom always used to tell us, "An idle mind is the devil's workshop." Chubie's goal metamorphosed from being a "choo choo" train driver to being a neurosurgeon. Funny, but at least he had a dream, a vision, a goal, and that's what is important. And my daughter, who wants to be a dentist, once had a goal of working at McDonald's so she could get free milkshakes.

Another revelation I have had about teenagers is this: Teenagers love and crave attention (Don't we all?). Years ago, in addition to my once-a-month date with my sweetheart, I decided to start taking each of my children out on a "just me and Mom" day once every month. With my daughter, we get our hair and nails done, go to the mall, hang out, and just chill. With my boys, we go to movies or to lunch or dinner. This is a wonderful time for relaxed communication without competition or interruption. Yes, no phone calls. Believe me, the most introverted teen will open up and talk to you about anything and everything in a relaxed setting. I have seen some good results from these "counseling sessions." Mothers, listen to me; our teenagers who have dedicated their lives to God need to know that they are still normal and okay in this immoral age of on-demand and free sex, drugs, and pornography. This has been a learning period both for my children and me. I am being made aware of what is out there. I think I am a better mom because I am knowledgeable about what it means to be a teenager in the twenty-first century. Teenagers have a lot in their minds to share, and they are yearning for us to listen. This time has also given me the opportunity to share with my children the fun memories of my own teenage years. Of course, I used to be a teen too, although my children look at my pictures from back then and tell me that I was a "geek."

I am having fun mothering these teenagers—praise the Lord! Stop listening to all those negative voices in society today that label our lovely teens as terrible, awful, appalling, dreadful, horrible, and horrendous. While we are still talking about our lovely and wonderful "walking hormones"—oops, I mean teenagers, allow me to delve into an area very crucial in teenagers' lives: to date or not to date. Let me say this again, the right time for dating is only after marriage. "What do you mean, Stella? How am I supposed to know who to marry if I don't date?" My answer is loud and clear, "I didn't date before marriage, but God, the best matchmaker, gave me Jerry, the best husband in the whole wide world."

Before I go on, I like to bring some clarity to how I am using the word "dating" in this book. I am referring to dating as "premarital dating"—dating before marriage. So when I say that the right time for dating is only after marriage, I mean postmarital dating. By postmarital dating, I mean those special times a husband and wife spend together to reconnect and recharge their romance.

To date or not to date? These are issues that require some thoughtful consideration, so let's pause here to give these issues of premarital dating and courtship a Christian viewpoint. However, a word of caution here. I do understand that some women have made some wrong judgments either in their own lives or in the lives of their children. God is aware of that, and the most assuring and comforting revelation is that He still loves you. But He loves you so much that He does not want you to keep making the same wrong decisions.

Even Christian parents have challenged me several times because they don't understand how their teenagers and young adult children can find their marriage partners if they don't date before marriage. All I tell them is that when they encourage their children to date before marriage, they are giving them the perfect license to have sex before marriage (Case closed!). "And what's wrong with that, sex before marriage? After all, we are living in the twenty-first century," you ask. Again, my answer is loud and clear: The last time I checked, sex before and outside of marriage is still a sin (1 Corinthians 6:9). Mothers, listen. God cannot be mocked (Galatians 6:7). You are learning how to be a mother after the heart of God. It is high time we started sowing the right seeds in our children's lives. Because everybody is doing it doesn't make it right.

Dating before marriage is like shopping; it does not lead to a marriage partner but to premarital sex, pain, disappointment, and heartbreak. Dating before marriage is like going to the mall to buy a shirt, knowing very well that there is a customer-satisfaction-guaranteed policy attached to the purchase. You go home, you try the shirt, maybe wear it a couple of times, and if you decide for any reason that you don't like it anymore, you can return it to the store. The reason to take the shirt back to the store may even be because you found another color or style that you like better. The only difference here is that in premarital dating, you are dealing with someone's mind, heart, and soul. I talk to teenagers and young adults all the time, and I get to hear about the nasty pain, heartaches, and rejections that come from dating. This is not the plan God has for His children; this is not the abundant life He promised us in John 10:10.

Now, let's talk about courtship. God has put in place a way to find a marriage partner; it is called God-Centered Courtship (GCC). Oh yes, go ahead, call me old-fashioned, it won't be the first or the last time. I know I am not old-fashioned, I am just God-fashioned … get it? And you all wonder why many marriages end the way they do. It is because they did not start the way God intended them to start.

"Is this a Catholic thing?"

No!

"Is this an African thing?"

No!

The questions I am asked every day are indeed very amazing. Courtship is a God thing. Please note that courtship is not Christian dating.

I have been asked many times, "What does court-ship look like? How is it different from Christian dating?" Let's not play around with words. This so-called "Christian dating" has led many of our children and young adults to a lot of anxiety, disappointment, and pain. This is because Christian dating is still premarital dating. Unlike courtship, which is based on God's wisdom, premarital dating (whether by Christians or non-Christians) is based on man's wisdom. One of the wisdoms behind premarital dating is to have "certain needs" met until the right marriage partner is found. In this process of having "certain needs" met, premarital dating creates a fake and false oneness between the two people involved. This false oneness results in the terrible pain and heartache experienced when the dating relationship ends. I talk to a lot of teenagers and young adults, and I see all the broken hearts and hurt feelings. This issue of false oneness is a very important one, because this is one of the huge differences between premarital dating and courtship. In courtship, you spend time together to get to know each other, but you stay away from activities that will stimulate sexual intimacy. You avoid the occasions that will promote ungodly choices and behavior. Because premarital dating focuses more on time spent alone with each other, it tends to be more self-centered than God-centered. As Christians, anything that is not God-centered is detrimental to our witness. From my viewpoint, the term "Christian dating" is a misnomer. Why would a Christian get involved in something that violates God's principles?

Another huge difference between premarital dating and courtship is that in premarital dating, there is no accountability. The accountability is an essential and vital factor in courtship. The two people in courtship must, and I repeat, must have a mature Christian couple who they will be accountable to. This could be either or both sets of parents of the two individuals. Where either or both sets of parents are not available to act as accountability couples, this would be a trusted, godly couple. Jerry and I have been an accountability couple many times. Accountability is an important part of our everyday life, at home, at work, and at church.

"What is courtship?" God-centered courtship is a process of seeking God's will and choice in selecting your marriage partner. Note the key words: God's will and God's choice. Courtship is praying, "God, I will your will and I choose your choice in my marriage partner." In courtship, it's all about God's will and His choice for you. It is not about you and your physical, emotional, and psychological needs. In courtship you do all things:

A. Heartily unto God (Colossians 3:23)

B. To the glory of God (1 Corinthians 10:31)

C. In the name of Jesus (Colossians 3:17)

D. Without offense to your testimony (1 Corinthians 8:13).

First Timothy 1:5 says, "But the aim of such instruction is love that comes from a pure heart, a good conscience, and sincere faith." Again, note the keywords: purity, good conscience, and sincere faith. First Timothy 4:12 says, "Let no one despise your youth, but set the believers an example in speech and conduct, in love, in purity and in faith." These letters were written to Timothy, a young person like our teenagers and young adults.

Marriage, as we all know, is a sacred thing that will not only affect your life here in this world but also in the world to come. Personally, I think it is much better to let God help you *build* your marriage than to go to Him for repairs. God is the best match-maker, not premarital dating; premarital dating is only a match-breaker. A right marriage will result from a right courtship. A God-centered courtship that is honorably conducted and prayerfully engaged will not terminate as a mistaken marriage.

A God-centered courtship does not start until a young man or woman has taken time to develop his/her identity in God. Also, before a young adult goes into courtship, he/she should have taken some time to get some education or training in the field of his/her interest. They have to be able to sustain their family. This is the time for the young adult to get busy in the Lord's vineyard, in one ministry or another, being good stewards of their time, talents, and treasure. This is the time to grow and develop spiritually, physically, emotionally, and psychologically while building healthy, godly friendships.

God, in His wisdom, instituted the sacrament of marriage. Our problem is that we think we know more than God. As a young adult develops godly friendships and seeks God's will and choice in a marriage partner, he/she will trust in the Lord with all his/her heart and will not rely on his/her understanding (Proverbs 3:5). Our young adults should continue with their earnest prayers while looking out for any clues that God may give them as they position themselves for His will in this matter. Mothers, encourage your children to seek your advice or the advice of one or two Christian people who know them well to discuss the possibilities. They should never be in a hurry.

God is eternal and is never in a hurry. God may not show up when and how we want Him to, but He has never missed an appointment. If God keeps our children waiting for an answer, there is a reason for it. Advise them to be patient. "One who trusts will not panic" (Isaiah 28:16b). An old adage says, "Marry in haste and repent at leisure." In the meantime, they should strive to develop those godly qualities that another good Christian man or woman will look for in a marriage partner. Good begets good.

During courtship, you will start spending time together, being very careful to avoid activities that will "stir up or awaken love until it is ready!" (Song of Solomon 2:7) Because courtship is God-centered and unlike premarital dating, which concentrates on time spent all alone with each other, courting concentrates on time spent together with friends and families. You have heard about the phrase "Location, Location, Location" in business. In courtship, it is also about location, location, location! The two individuals should avoid being alone in isolated locations, because they know they are to be very, very careful to develop a friendship that will honor God in its entirety.

For this is the will of God, your sanctification: that you abstain from fornication, that each one of you know how to control your own body in holiness and honor. Not with lustful passion, like the gentiles who do not know God, that no one wrong or exploit a brother or sister in this matter, because the Lord is an avenger in all these things, just as we have already told you beforehand and solemnly warned you. For God did not call us to impurity but in holiness. Therefore whoever rejects this rejects not human authority but God who also gives His Holy Spirit to you.

1 Thessalonians 4:3–8

Now, my dear mothers, we have a lot of accounting to give to God in regards to how we have nurtured our children. Nurturing and teaching our children that true love really waits is part of our job as a homemaker. Please, please take time to teach your children about God's intention in marital love. Marital love encompasses friendship love, sexual love, and self-giving love. In courtship, only the friendship love is developed; the sexual and self-giving love are reserved for marriage. But premarital dating focuses on physical attraction and a fake physical oneness, a cheap and imitation physical oneness. Love and sexual union are God-given privileges for a man and woman to share in the context of marriage. Sexual fulfillment and enjoyment between marriage partners are part of God's good design for us. My darling mothers, will you take a stand with me today? Let's dig in our heels together and take a very unpopular stand in today's culture, stand to save our children from the horrible jaws of immorality. Remember: "United we stand, but divided we fall."

Spiritual Motherhood

I want to say something here about an important issue God put in my heart many, many years ago. I want to talk about spiritual motherhood, because I believe that this ideal mother extends her teaching and nurturing to other boys and girls who aren't her own natural sons and daughters. My first experience as a spiritual mother started over ten years ago in an encounter with a young girl who was having some problems in her life. I became very good friends with her, and she opened up to me. I introduced her to my family, and she is the first of my spiritual sons and daughters. My three children were at her wedding. As I write this book, I am getting ready to go spend a night with one of my spiritual mothers. She is an eighty-three-year-old widow who has no natural children and is terminally ill. Mamasita Margarita has and continues to nurture me in all areas of my life, especially in the area of being a submissive wife.

Another word for spiritual motherhood is mentoring. When I read the story of Esther in the Bible, I marvel at what mentoring can produce. Remember Esther, one of the Jewish minorities in Persia, was a peasant orphan girl who God raised from nothing— from obscurity to become the queen of Persia. Do you know that people will seldom reach their destiny without a mentor? Mentoring is a huge thing now in many colleges across the country. Social workers are always looking for mentors for children in foster homes, underprivileged children, and children of minority background.

There cannot be an Esther without a Mordecai. Esther was Mordecai's cousin whom Mordecai took in as his own daughter when her father and mother died. I strongly recommend that you read chapter two of the Book of Esther to see how mentoring can and does change a life. Look around your family, extended family, your church community, your neighborhood, or your children's school community and see if there is a young boy or girl, a single father, perhaps an unwed mom who needs some spiritual guidance. A friend of mine describes mentoring as picking up the little birds that have flown out of the nest and putting them back in.

Ladies, we are born to mother and nurture. A note of warning here: Spiritual motherhood is not always nice and sweet. Just as it is with our own natural children, it takes a lot of love, patience, and prayers (LPP). If you have ever had a baby before, you know about the agony, pain, and sweating involved in labor and delivery. The transition period is the hardest. It is not only hard; it is ugly, bitter, and dark. But because of the love you have for your baby, you just don't give up; you continue to push all the way until that baby is born, and then the joy, the happiness, the smiles, the tears, and the laughter follow. So it is with spiritual motherhood. When you go through the transition phase, you have to love the person enough with the love of Jesus so that you don't give up. I have been tempted to give up many times, but I refused. I always remind myself that my spiritual sons and daughters don't have to like me to get what is inside of me. I just have to continue loving them, continue being patient with them, and continue praying for them (LPP). My worst battles with my spiritual sons and daughters have been in areas of sexual immorality. I don't know how to dress up words. I call it as it is. I don't play games. Again, we cannot give up, and just like our own children, we love them, pray for them, and just be patient.

So, my dear ladies, be open to God and watch Him bless you with spiritual sons and daughters. As for me, the one thing God has raised me up with a mantle to do is to equip and train young ambassadors for Christ. I have been blessed with a number of spiritual sons and daughters. I thank God for His grace and guidance as I work with these teenagers and young adults—our young ambassadors for Christ.

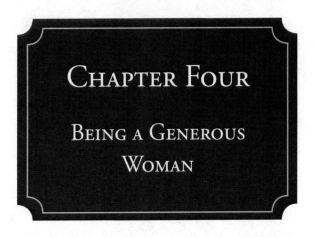

CHAPTER FOUR

BEING A GENEROUS WOMAN

"She opens her hand to the poor, and reaches out her hands to the needy."

Proverbs 31:20

Our friend is a generous woman. She has the splendid grace of giving. She is a blesser. This woman is aware of God's will concerning our relationship to the poor and needy among us, as He commanded in Deuteronomy 15:11, "Since there will never cease to be some in need on the earth, I therefore command you. Open your hand to the poor and needy in your land."

What I really like most about her generosity is that she is the initiator. Proverbs 31:20 tells us that she "reaches out" her hands to the poor and needy. "You mean that she does not wait for an appeal letter to come from her pastor or priest to give?" She does not wait for Christmas to be in the spirit of giving. She actually takes the first step in reaching out to help the poor, the needy, the hungry, the orphans, and widows.

Last year a friend of ours lost his wife to cancer, and when I overheard my dear husband saying to his grieving friend on the phone, "Please call me if you need me," I just about jumped out of my skin. *Men...* I thought. Then I quietly calmed myself down, faked a smile, and lovingly (remember, I am still in training) advised my husband to go over to the man's home and just be there for him. There are times when all we need to give is our presence, not a sermon or even a Bible verse. We should be searching for ways to reach out to the poor, the needy, and those hurting among us.

Our ideal woman is not selfish. She is a very compassionate woman. She has a sincere caring for others. Compassion is almost becoming an extinct virtue in today's "me, myself, and I" culture. Today's culture says, "Get all you can and sit on the lid." We cannot be good stewards of our time, talents, and treasure without being compassionate. It is compassion that drives us to volunteer at a homeless shelter. It is compassion for the lonely that drives us to visit the shutins in our neighborhood. Jesus is a very compassionate savior, father, and friend. The Bible tells us that He wept at a friend's funeral (John 11:35). His compassion was manifested toward the crowd in Mark 6:34: "As he went ashore, he saw a great crowd, and he had compassion for them, because they were like sheep without a shepherd, and he began to teach them many things."

Jesus' compassion caused Him to be very concerned for the physical needs of the people. He asked where to buy bread for the people to eat (John 6:5). His compassion led Him to heal the blind (Matthew 20:34), cure the poor lepers (Mark 1:41), and liberate those possessed by demons (Luke 4:41). Jesus spoke and spent time with the Samaritans, who were looked down upon at that time by the Jews. He accepted women as disciples in a culture where women were second-class citizens. He even ate with sinners. *Wow!* Talk about being compassionate and demonstrating your compassion with actions.

My dear ladies, let us learn to love in both word and in deed. Let us learn to be generous of our time, talents, and treasure. The need around us could be financial, emotional, spiritual, physical, or psychological. Our new lady friend from Proverbs has a genuine concern for the people in need. Instead of helping from a distance, she opens her arms and extends her hands. This woman is willing to be involved personally. She makes a deliberate attempt to reach out to the hurting, the miserable, the forgotten, the oppressed, the suffering, the lonely, the sick, and the discriminated against. May the Holy Spirit help us to "open our arms and extend our hands" to make the world a better place.

Jerry was a soccer coach for over twenty years. One year we had a young boy who had just immigrated to the United States with his family. This young boy loved to play soccer, but his parents could not afford to pay for his uniforms and team fees. All the parents pitched in and got the boy his uniform and paid his team fees. What you make happen for others God will make happen for you.

My mom and dad are in their midseventies and are currently raising two teenagers who are not related to us. My parents have already raised six of their own natural children and over twenty children who are either nieces or nephews. About fifteen years ago, a single father was living in a shack with his children. This single father was unemployed, and his wife had just left him and their children. To help him out, my parents would have him do some yard work for them as needed. But as the children grew older, my parents sensed the danger they faced in getting involved with the wrong crowd while living on the streets. After a period of prayers and discernment, my parents took these kids in to live with them. The girl, who was five years old at that time, is now in college with a major in pharmacy, and the boy, who was three at that time, is now in high school.

God's people are expected to remain faithful and obedient to Him, and part of that obedience is caring for the needs of the poor around us. We don't all have to go to the extent my parents went to with these children, but we can start by first being willing to keep our compassionate eyes open. Our compassionate eyes are not our natural eyes, but the eyes of our heart.

I always tell my children never to look down on anybody (*anybody!*) unless they are picking them up. That is the only way to be on the lookout, with your eyes of compassion open. You may be called to help the son of a working single mom with a ride to and from his basketball games, or to sponsor a child from Africa, Croatia, India, Mexico, or South America. Get your children involved too. Your children could babysit free of charge for a married couple to go out on a date once in a while. A single dad may need someone to babysit his children once or twice a week so that he can work out in the gym. Your son or daughter may decide to volunteer at the Boys and Girls Club to tutor once a week. We should develop and expose our children to numerous opportunities for them to give of their talents, treasure, and time.

Don't you want to see your children in heaven? I do! My children know how much my husband and I want to see them in heaven. You have to desire to make a mark for God in your children's lives. You are an agent on assignment, an undercover secret service agent for God. What will be your legacy when you die? What are you handing down to your children? Sometimes we are overly cautious about expos- ing our children to the real world out there, and I always wonder why. How do we expect our children to grow up being compassionate if we have not taken the time to sow that seed? There is always seed time and harvest time. The earlier we start sowing these seeds, the better for our children. I always tell parents, "Catch them young for Jesus and they will never stray." And even if they stray, they will always come back to God. An utmost God will not have an almost child! Proverbs 22:6 says, "Train children in the right way and when old, they will not stray."

Most of the time, my dear ladies, it is not that we are doing something wrong; it is that we are not doing enough of the right stuff. One day, as we all know, it won't matter how much money you have or how many degrees you have attached to your name; the only thing that will matter is your response to the question: "What did you do to the least of my children?" My three children have seen poverty up close and personal. During our visits to Nigeria, Jerry and I made sure we spent some time in the village after having fun in the big cities. The time spent in the villages has helped my children to appreciate hunger, disease, and despondency fully and on a higher level.

My children have played with kids who ran around in their underwear because they have only one piece of clothing, their dress, pants, or shirt worn only on Sundays for church. My children have come home to eat dinner with children who have not had breakfast or lunch but have been sent out hungry to play with other children in the neighborhood so that their parents could "buy time," hoping for a miraculous dinner. This is a good experience, a very humbling one. This is seed time, time to sow the seed of humility and uproot the weed of arrogance, and time to sow the seed of awareness and uproot the weed of ignorance. Do you know that arrogance and ignorance at the same time are the recipe for "killer cocktail," a very serious and dangerous combination?

Allow me to share a portion of my two sons' college application essays with you. Somutoo writes about his experience in Nigeria:

> Here I saw hunger manifested on the flesh of the children. Some children have hardly eaten for a number of days. They feel and look very fragile, their heads and stomachs have become distended. The children are vulnerable to disease. Diarrhea and typhoid take their toll because of lack of clean water and proper hygiene education. It was a demoralizing sight, but I was touched.

And Chubie writes,

> Today, my motto in life is to live simply, so that others can simply live. We are richly blessed in this country (U.S.A.), and yet we complain a lot about everything. I am more appreciative of the common things in life, things I used to take for granted, like crayons, coloring books, underwear, or a toothbrush. I don't have to own all the name-brand jeans or sneakers to be happy. I have learned

that being content with what I have is the first step to being compassionate in today's culture of greed. Being compassionate has set the nostalgia of a sincere caring for others in my heart. I now have this overpowering drive to look for ways to serve and to give, whether it is a classmate, a total stranger, the homeless in my community, or the desperately poor children back home in Nigeria.

What a powerful testimony! Jerry and I did not know that our sons would write about their experiences in Nigeria in their college application essays respectively. Those words brought tears to my eyes and joy to my heart. God says in Hosea 4:6, "My people are destroyed for lack of knowledge." Are your children being destroyed today for lack of knowledge about God's will concerning our relationship to the poor and the needy among us? Are your children even aware of the poor and the needy among us, both here in United States and overseas? Do your children know that God wants us to be extensions of His hands and legs?

My dear mothers, grandmothers, aunties, and sisters, let us all take time to sow the seed of compassion in our children today, so that they will grow up to be like Jesus—compassionate, merciful, kind, humble, meek, gentle, patient, and loving. Isn't this what Jesus is trying to teach us in the Beatitudes (Mark 5:3–11)? I call these "Kingdom-citizen characteristics." Remember, we are raising ambassadors for Christ (2 Corinthians 5:20) and future citizens of heaven (Philippians 3:20).

I believe that although God loves all of His children, He has a softspot for His generous children. God has a softspot for His good stewards. Good stewardship involves more than giving to God's work. It also involves helping meet the needs of the poor and the needy. The generous person who lovingly enjoys helping others is blessed abundantly. Proverbs 11:25 says, "A generous person will be enriched and one who gives water will get water." Proverbs 22:9 says, "Those who are generous are blessed for they share their bread with the poor." When we love God, everything we do should be to build lives of eternal consequences. Touch a soul today; lots of hugs and kisses will await you in heaven!

CHAPTER FIVE

BEING GOAL-ORIENTED & A WOMAN OF PURPOSE

"She perceives that her merchandise is profitable. Her lamp does not go out at night."

Proverbs 31:18

Planning ahead is the key to getting what you want in life. It takes some planning and organization to make a good home. Note: I did not say to "run" a good home. My dear ladies, we are homemakers not "home runners." Do you have a mission statement for your family? What goals do you as a family hope to accomplish tomorrow, this week, this month, or this year? Do your children know what your daily, weekly, and monthly expectations from them are? Do they have their own individual daily, weekly, monthly, and yearly goals?

I just came back from our yearly women's retreat, and I learned that every family is a little church. What is your little church like? Organized, focused, and goal-oriented, or confused, chaotic, and without direction? Are the choices you are making today in your little church getting you the results you want? Proverbs 31:25 tells us that our ideal woman friend "can laugh at the days to come." You know why? Because she has carefully planned and prepared for the future. Planning for the future goes beyond just financial planning.

A lot of women put in more time and energy planning a roadtrip than they do planning for their future and their family's future. Before a roadtrip, they lay out their itinerary and plan for the trip ahead of time. If they don't have a *GPS* (global positioning system) in their van, they quickly go to MapQuest to get directions to where they are going. They plan ahead of time where to stop and rest each day. They have a plan for what to do and what to see for every single day of the trip. They take the car in for a checkup, buy gas, pack enough food and drinks for the road, bring along their debit and credit cards, pack warm and cold clothing, and bring board games, iPods for the teenagers, and DVDs for their toddlers. All these plans just for a roadtrip, and they tend to forget to plan for the most important road-trip their family will ever take—*Life!*

Life is a very rigorous roadtrip, a journey with hills, valleys, and detours. Like all journeys, life needs a plan too. We just cannot go through life waking up and taking each day as it comes. We have to have a plan, a roadmap to take us to where we want to go in life. Without a plan, we cannot refocus our direction when we run into detours in order to get to our destination. And if you don't know where you are going, you won't know when you get there! Without a plan, we cannot take time to see what is needed at every leg of the journey to make provisions for those needs.

Every family needs to have a mission statement. All corporations and organizations in the world have a mission statement. My husband works for Boeing Company, and they have a mission statement. My office has a mission statement. A family's mission statement gives the members of the family identity. It also gives them direction and purpose. With direction and purpose, a family sets goals and makes plans to accomplish their goals. Also, the individual member of the family needs to have their own life goals and purpose. Although I don't claim to be an authority in writing mission statements, I am willing to share with you what has helped me and my family. A mission statement must have these three elements in it: a vision, purpose, and goals.

A vision is a mental picture of your "future you," an image of your future that's in your mind. Having a vision is very important in setting life goals and purpose. Even in dentistry, we use vision to motivate our patients toward taking good care of their teeth and gums. I always ask my patients to tell me where they see their teeth and gums five, ten years from now. You must be able to look into the future of your life, your family, your career, your business, or your ministry and form a mental impression of it. What do you think God was trying to teach Abraham when He took him outside and said, "Raise your eyes now, and look from the place where you are, northward, and southward, and eastward and westward; for all the land that you see I will give to you and to your offspring forever" (Genesis 13:14–15)? God was telling Abraham to develop a mental representation of the future of his life and that of his family. It is called foresight. Vision always has something to do with the future. If you can look into the future to see the invisible, God will do the impossible. I learned this from my dad, who started as a nobody to become a somebody. Born in 1934 into a very poor pagan polygamous family in Nigeria, with all odds against him, all he had was a big vision and a very big God. A person without a vision is like a fire without its light.

A purpose is what you hope to be. You cannot aim at being what you have not visualized. This is why vision is very important. Then the goals are the actions you have to take, the things you have to do to get to your purpose (what you hope to be). Success is not accidental but intentional. There is a relationship between your actions and your direction, your goals and your purposes. Is what you are doing today getting you where you are going? Do you have lined-up plans that will get you to your life goals? Do you have a plan for a successful marriage? Do you have a plan for a successful career, a successful business, a successful ministry? Have a plan and work your plan. If you work your plan, your plan will work for you. When we fail at some things in life, most of the time it is not because we planned to fail, it is because we failed to plan.

So, my dear friends, be legacy minded, start teaching your children, your grandchildren, your nieces, your nephews, and your cousins how to have a vision, life purpose, and life goals. You see, children are like catapults in the hands of their parents, grandparents, aunties, and sisters. What use is a catapult if you don't aim it at something? Aim your children at something high and position them for success. Teach them early in life to dream big and to understand that the limitations they have will not stop them from reaching their goals because they can do all things through Christ who gives them strength (Philippians 4:13). Teach them that it is not by their power nor by their might, but by God's Sprit as He promised in Zechariah 4:6. I always tell my children to work hard, dream big, and trust God! And what is our ultimate life goal? Our ultimate life goal should be to get to heaven—to spend eternity loving God.

Even Jesus, our master, had a life goal when he was here on earth: "For the son of man came to seek out and to save the lost" (Luke 19:10). His mission is to lead people to a saving relationship with God, a personal, intimate, and loving relationship that will deliver people from their sinful ways and lifestyles and lead them to the service of God and other people. With His life goal in mind, Jesus was able to stay organized, focused, and centered when He ran into the road bumps, the hills, valleys, and detours on His life journey. Focus is everything. Focus helps you to say no even to a good thing if it is not in agreement with your vision, your purpose, and your goal. At the mountain of Transfiguration, when Jesus took His select team up the mountain to see Him in His full glory, Peter came up with a brilliant idea: "Lord, it is good for us to be here, if you wish, I will make three dwellings here, one for you, one for Moses, and one for Elijah" (Matthew 17:5). But Jesus knew He had to get down the mountain. He was focused on His life goal of seeking and saving the lost.

So now, to the million-dollar question of the year: Are your footsteps being ordered by God, being in the right place at the right time as you take your most important long and winding roadtrip? Let's break the power of old habits as you step into a new season in your life. Your reading this book at this particular time in your life is not a coincidence but a God-incidence. You are getting ready to step into a new and very important season in your life, "a put off/put on" season, a season to put off old habits and to put on new habits. After all, that's the idea behind this book, the reason why we have decided to hang out with this, our newfound friend—Mrs. Proverbs 31.

"Okay, enough said. Stella, let's get practical. How do I go about writing my life goals and purpose?" Fine, I am going to share with you how I did mine, and you can go from there. My life goals and purpose are written under three distinctive subtitles: God first, family second, and others third.

God first: Remember the Bible verse, "Strive first for the Kingdom of God and His righteousness, and all these things will be given to you as well" (Matthew 6:33). My pastor, Father Tom, will always remind us to keep the main thing the main thing. My first life goal is to major in the *Major.* It's time for you to stop majoring in the minor and minoring in the major. My primary goal every day is to wear Jesus as a perfume, so that when I walk into a room, even the blind can "see" Jesus in me. I want Christ to shine forth in all that I do, say, or think in all my daily contacts at home, work, church, at the grocery store, the post office, the bank, the soccer field, the movie theater, the mall, the dance floor, the restaurant, the prayer meeting, and so on.

Family second: This is where all my personal and my family life goals and purpose come under.

Others third: This includes my career and my ministry goals and purpose.

To help you realize your goals and purpose, it helps to break them down into daily, weekly, monthly, and yearly goals. Some of my weekly goals are: to spend a miracle hour with Jesus in the Blessed Eucharist chapel, to pre-cook the week's dinners ahead for the freezer, to go through my intercessory prayer list, and encourage some friends by either calling them or writing them.

The whole point is to have some direction in your life daily, weekly, monthly, and yearly, so you will be able to control your days and weeks instead of letting them control you. You may be feeling so overwhelmed now and don't even know how and where to start; I completely understand. Why don't you start by getting a pen and paper and prayerfully ask God to help you do what honors Him the most tomorrow under these three subtitles: God, family, and others. Write them down, and there goes your daily goals for tomorrow. Start small by making daily goals, then weekly goals, then monthly goals, and before you know it, you will have your yearly goals in front of you. Keep in mind, there will be days when all your plans will fall apart. On such days, the loving thing to do is to abandon your goals for those days and still thank God for the gift of those days.

Remember, you cannot do this by yourself; you need to pray constantly over your goals and purpose, and you need to call upon the Holy Sprit to help you. God is ready and willing to teach you if you call upon Him. "Who are they that fear the Lord, He will teach them the way that they should choose" (Psalm 25:12).

When you become a goal-oriented woman, you will begin to appreciate the gift of every second of the minute, every minute of the hour, and every hour of each day of your life. You will begin to realize that you can no longer afford to sit around and be lazy or waste an hour watching *Desperate Housewives.* This ideal woman of Proverbs 31 "looks well to the ways of her house hold, and does not eat the bread of idleness" (verse 27). See, I told you, she is very organized, focused, and goal oriented.

When you become focused and goal oriented, there will be a paradigm shift in your mind, and your brain will start thinking in terms of seconds and minutes. Each second, each minute is a precious gift from God, and you cannot afford to take it for granted. Believe me, I totally know what I am saying. If you have not read my first book, please get a copy of it today, and your life will never be the same. In my first book titled "A Walk through the Dark Valley of Death," I wrote about my near-death experience. I went from being very healthy to being in a septic shock and coma in a matter of days. I learned a very huge lesson. I will never take any second of my life for granted again. Never!

It's never too late to start being organized, goal oriented, and a woman of purpose. Start today. It does not matter how disorganized and chaotic your life has been in the past and still is right now. It's never too late to turn a new leaf. The remaining part of your life is what matters most now. If you didn't start well, you can still finish well. God is more interested in your future than He is in your past. Always remember this: Knowledge is not power; applied knowledge is power. The knowing is just half of it, only half of the "enchilada." What you do with what you know is where the power lies.

CHAPTER SIX

CELEBRATE YOUR BEAUTY

"She makes herself coverings; her clothing is fine linen and purple."

Proverbs 31:22

It is very important to know that as a woman of God, it does not matter if you are in the lunch-room or the laundry room, in high heels or hight-ops, a CEO or a SHM (stay-at-home mom). You are still God's classy woman and need to celebrate your beauty. Pricilla, in Acts 18, was a career woman who made tents with her husband, and Mary, John Mark's mother in Acts 12:12, was a stay-at-home mother, but both women blossomed where God planted them for their names to be in the Bible. It does not matter if you are single or married, young or old; you are still God's classy woman, and you need to celebrate your beauty. Remember, "Charm is deceitful, and [external] beauty is vain, but a woman who fears the Lord is to be praised" (Proverbs 31:30.) Lydia, in Acts 16:11–14, was a single woman; Anna, the prophet in Luke 2:36, was an old woman; our Blessed Mother Mary was only a teenager. All these women certainly bloomed where God planted them for them to be a critical part of Christianity right from its beginnings.

When you think of a flower blooming in your garden, what comes to your mind first is what you see with your eyes—the visual is very important to me. I will spend some time to talk about celebrating your beauty in this last chapter. If you have ever met me in person, you will know that there is no way I would write a book on being an ideal woman and not spend some time talking about your beauty as you blossom in your own part of God's garden. Our outer beauty depends on our inner beauty, which comes from knowing we are loved. When you reflect this inner beauty, people will compliment you by saying, "There's a glow about you…"

Most of your looks are all in your grooming. The Proverbs 31 woman takes very good care of herself. She is indeed a perfect advertisement of God's goodness, a posterwoman of God. Verse 22 tells us that "her clothing is fine linen and purple." In case you don't know, this was the clothing of the wealthy during that time. I tell you, this woman knows how to look good. She is my kind of Christian woman; the look good, feel good, healthy Christian woman. She is what I call a "Correct Sista." I am not telling you to start heading to Nordstrom now. That's not the point. The point is not the expensive clothing but the nice, clean, sharp clothing. Nice, clean, and sharp do not have to be expensive.

I am a strong believer in looking good for God. If the unbeliever-woman knows how to take good care of herself to look good for the unbelieving world, I can and should look better by God's standards because I am a princess, a daughter of the Most High God, the Kings of kings. *Hello!* I don't believe that because I am a Christian, I should walk around looking sorry, sloppy, and dowdy. *No way!* Whoever came up with the idea that Christians should not look good, sharp, nice, and classy for God? Do you know that part of your Christian influence in today's unbelieving world is how you look? I don't know about you, but I want unbelievers to look at me and say, "You know what? God *really works!*" Psalm 92:12–15 confirms,

The righteous flourish like the palm tree and grow like a cedar in Lebanon. They are planted in the house of the Lord; they flourish in the courts of our God. In old age they still produce

fruit, they are always green and full of sap, showing that the Lord is upright.

You see, my dear friend, that's the very reason
to look good and sharp for Jesus, to show that He
is upright.

Every woman's wardrobe should be nice, clean,
and sharp but tailored to her calling in life. Remember that you should only bloom where God planted
you. Your wardrobe will be determined by the part
of God's garden you are planted in. If God planted
you in the countryside and you are a farmer, fine, go
ahead and look nice and sharp in your jeans for Jesus
and still blossom to draw other farmers to Jesus.
This is what I mean by tailoring your wardrobe to
your calling in life.

You should reflect the beauty of a woman whose
life is centered in God. I know talking about out-
ward beauty in some Christian circles is like treading
on dangerous ground, and I don't understand why.
Inasmuch as I need to be ministered to spiritually
and mentally, I need to be ministered to physically

too. You think Jesus walked around ungroomed? I don't think so. Your hair, your face, eyes, nails, hands, legs, and feet should be well groomed and should look good to the glory of God. Your whole body, from the crown of your head to the soles of your feet, should be clean and healthy to the glory of God. Is this not what living from the inside out means? So why do some Christian women only work on the inside and forget about the outside? You should take care of your outside too, to reflect the beauty of God inside of you. What is the point of taking good care of your inner beauty and neglecting your outer beauty? To become more spiritual does not mean to neglect your outer beauty. Your outer beauty is very important, because unbelievers look into the mirror of your outer beauty to see this Jesus that you talk about. It's just like when I go shopping; the window displays in some of the shops lure me into the store. That's the whole idea behind beautiful window displays. You (as a woman of God) are a spiritual window display, so take some time to celebrate your beauty.

I want people to see me and see God in my inner woman and also in my outer woman. I want to influence people toward God by every single means I can think of, and part of it is in my beauty. I try to stay healthy by watching what I eat and drink and by exercising. I jog three or four miles every day, and I drink eight to ten cups of water daily. Do you know that you can not do the work God has called you to do if you are not healthy? Always think healthy to get wealthy, and I don't mean wealthy in monetary terms. I mean the wealth of love, joy, peace, patience, kindness, generosity, faithfulness, gentleness, and self-control, the fruit of the Hoy Spirit (Galatians 5:22). You cannot operate fully in the fruit if you are constantly tired and unhealthy. Think about it, if you are always tired, the odds are that you are always grouchy and easily irritated. You will tend to lose your cool very easily, and nobody, not even your best friend, husband, or children will want to be around you because you are just always grouchy. No one wants to hang out with a "bitter pill." If your family cannot stand to be around you, can you even begin to imagine what your friends, co-workers, associates, colleagues, clients, or patients are thinking? And you are supposed to be the Christian, their salt and their light. How on earth can you tell them about Jesus if they cannot stand your guts?

My dear sister and friend, my dear woman of God, take another look at yourself. It does not have to cost you a lot of money to take good care of yourself. You do not have to dress up in "fine linen and purple," the expensive stuff, to look clean, nice, and sharp for God. Your body is the temple of the Holy Spirit; take good care of your body in every single aspect of it, from your hair to your toes. Let your beauty be part of the way you represent God in your family, church, community, and at work. You are a spiritual window display, a commercial, an advertisement of God's loving care, mercy, and kindness to His children.

This Proverbs 31 woman has taught us a lot of good and godly things. We know she has both inner and outer beauty because she took the time each day to feed her spirit, soul, and body to the glory of God. Are you willing to start feeding your spirit, soul, and body today in like manner, to the glory of God? God is saying this to you right now, "This day I call heaven and earth as witnesses against you that I have set before you life and death, blessings and curses. *Now Choose Life,* so that you and your children may live" (Deuteronomy 30:19).

How to Contact the Author

Congratulations and thank you for choosing life. Let me know how you are doing. Write me or visit my Web site: www.starbrightministries.com.

Please include your testimony or help received from this book when you write. Your prayer requests are welcome too. I may be contacted for speaking engagements at Stellannanabu@Starbrightministries.com.

ENDNOTES

1 (Novo Millennio Ineunte, 30).